OBJECT LESSONS

for

children

Luke

CHRISTIAN LIGHT

PUBLICATIONS

OBJECT LESSONS FOR CHILDREN
Christian Light Publications
Harrisonburg, Virginia 22802
©2020 Christian Light Publications, Inc.
Printed in the United States of America

ISBN: 978-0-87813-312-3

Cover & Interior Design: Elizabeth McMurray
Cover & Interior Graphics: Brandon Hartman, Getty Images

Contents

Compiler's Note

This book is a compilation of devotional lessons shared by the fathers and school board members of Jonestown Mennonite School, along with others gathered from various sources. It is intended to inspire ideas for devotions, children's meetings, Bible study lessons, and similar occasions. Each of the lessons could be applied and developed in various ways. Some are directly school-related, while others focus on Bible truths.

Jesus used object lessons: a fig tree, a coin, and a child. He spoke of taking an ax to the root of a tree, entering in at the strait gate, and letting our light shine like a candle on a candlestick. Many deep Bible truths are illustrated or taught by comparisons and contrasts to simple objects we use every day.

It is my desire that these ideas will serve as starters for great lessons that teach truth and inspire children to love God and obey Him. Put your mind to work, minding the Spirit of God, and consider what lessons you can share with children. Children love a good object lesson and will likely remember it for a long time.

Opportunities

Theme

We should learn everything we can in school while we have the opportunity.

Items you will need

- Water gun/soaker (Can be purchased inexpensively at a dollar store. Consider using a pump-style rather than a militant-looking gun.)
- Large bucket of water

Object lesson

Tell the students that the water represents things they can learn, and the water soaker represents them as students. Fill the soaker as full as possible to illustrate the fact that when you prepare for a water battle, you would be foolish to enter the game with a partially filled soaker.

- We each are like this soaker: we can fill ourselves with knowledge in preparation for life.
- School is an opportunity to fill up with knowledge and wisdom.

- We don't know what all we may need in life. We must prepare for anything that may come.
- A filled soaker can represent potential. How much potential do you have?

Verses to consider

Ecclesiastes 9:10—Whatsoever thy hand findeth to do, do it with thy might; for there is no work, nor device, nor knowledge, nor wisdom, in the grave, whither thou goest.

Proverbs 4:7—Wisdom is the principal thing; therefore get wisdom: and with all thy getting get understanding.

Proverbs 16:16—How much better is it to get wisdom than gold! and to get understanding rather to be chosen than silver!

Applications

How can you fill your soaker?

1. Come to school every day.
2. Pay attention in class and answer the teacher's questions.
3. Read and study the lesson completely.
4. Do your homework carefully. Double-check your answers.
5. Study diligently for tests.
6. Learn your Bible memory to fill your mind with verses for spiritual warfare.

7. Consider how school lessons apply to life outside of school.
8. Look up interesting things in the encyclopedia—learn from more than just your textbook.

Additional ideas

You could arrange with a student beforehand to help you by letting you splash them lightly with water. After filling up the soaker, tell the class your helper is going to get wet. Everyone will anticipate that you will soak them. You can simply use your fingers and flick some water on your helper.

If you are able to, discharge your soaker outside and show them how far it reaches.

My Cup Runneth Over

Theme

When we have joy and cheerfulness, we can share them with others.

Items you will need

- Three cups: one very small, one medium, one large
- A flat pan to catch water from the cups
- Enough water to fill the medium cup

Object lesson

Fill the medium cup with water before class. Pour the water from the medium cup into the little cup to show how this cup can easily make the little cup run over.

Leave the large cup empty, but ask the children how much they think this one would make the little cup run over. Then tell them the large cup represents Satan's offer to make us feel happy with things of the world that go against God, but it is all empty. Pour out of this large cup into the little cup and surprise them with there being nothing in it.

- Our hearts are our cups. Are they full and running over with joy?
- When our cups run over, they touch others and help fill their cups too.
- When you pour water back and forth between cups, you usually spill some and have less each time. With cheerfulness, the more you pour it into others, the more you have for yourself, even after sharing some with others nearby!

Verses to consider

Psalm 23:5—Thou preparest a table before me in the presence of mine enemies: thou anointest my head with oil; my cup runneth over.

Proverbs 27:19—As in water face answereth to face, so the heart of man to man. Paraphrase: *Like water mirrors our face back to us, so cheerfulness to others reflects back to us.*

Applications

1. Being cheerful brings cheer to others.
2. A smile often receives a smile back.
3. Joys shared are multiplied; joys kept to ourselves are reduced.
4. Satan tempts us with happiness for taking our own way instead of God's way, but it is an empty, false promise.

5. Smoking, alcohol, drugs, carnivals, and ungodly movies each promise lots of happiness, but are all empty!

6. David's cup was full and running over because he followed the Shepherd.

3

Yield Not to Temptation

Theme

Sin always brings negative consequences.

Items you will need

- A mouse trap and bait
- A ruler or stick
- Optional: A toy mouse

Object lesson

Begin by setting the trap while the children watch in expectation. Tell them the bait represents temptation—it looks so good to a mouse. But what happens when we give in to temptation and sin? You can then trip the trap with the ruler (or mouse, if you brought one).

- The Bible says the wages (payment or consequence) of sin is death.
- Sin looks tempting to us because it feels good to do in the moment. Satan tries to hide the consequences of sin from us.

- ○ The closer we get to sin, the more we wish for it and the harder it is to say no to it.
- ○ Sin always brings bad consequences.

Verses to consider

James 1:12—Blessed is the man that endureth temptation: for when he is tried, he shall receive the crown of life, which the Lord hath promised to them that love him.

James 1:14, 15—But every man is tempted, when he is drawn away of his own lust, and enticed. Then when lust hath conceived, it bringeth forth sin: and sin, when it is finished, bringeth forth death.

1 Corinthians 10:13—There hath no temptation taken you but such as is common to man: but God is faithful, who will not suffer you to be tempted above that ye are able; but will with the temptation also make a way to escape, that ye may be able to bear it.

Joshua 7—*The story of Achan yielding to temptation.*

Numbers 32:23—But if ye will not do so, behold, ye have sinned against the Lord: and be sure your sin will find you out.

Applications

Discuss some potential consequences of yielding to temptation in these examples:

1. Being tempted to lie to cover up when we disobeyed.

2. Being tempted to look at another person's paper for an answer.
3. Being tempted to take a cookie while Mother isn't watching.
4. Being tempted to show off or brag.

Additional ideas

You can write "LAW" on the edge of the trap and "CONSEQUENCES" on the back. You can use this to illustrate that all laws carry consequences for breaking them. The law is like a set trap, you break it and you pay!

○ Some people break the law to get attention.
○ Others don't like to submit to the law. They want to be their own boss.
○ Many think they can get by with lawbreaking and no one can catch them.

"Knowing this, that the law is not made for a righteous man, but for the lawless and disobedient, for the ungodly and for sinners, for unholy and profane, for murderers of fathers and murderers of mothers, for manslayers" (1 Timothy 1:9).

4

Pride

Theme

Pride brings destruction and embarrassment.

Items you will need

- Two balloons
- A straight pin
- A story about a boastful child

Object lesson

Use two balloons to illustrate pride. One balloon stays flat to illustrate a humble person. You can prick him with a pin, but he does not pop. Fill the other balloon with air to illustrate a proud person. Prick this one to show how pride brings destruction—*Pop!*

You can add interest by telling a story about a boastful child. You blow more air into the balloon with each big statement. As the character brags, you keep on blowing up the balloon until it pops.

- Pride is when we think we are bigger than we really are.
- Boasting is a form of pride.

○ Showing off is another form of pride.

Verses to consider

Proverbs 16:18—Pride goeth before destruction, and an haughty spirit before a fall.

Proverbs 11:2—When pride cometh, then cometh shame: but with the lowly is wisdom.

Proverbs 18:12—Before destruction the heart of man is haughty, and before honour is humility.

The Book of Esther—Haman's pride results in him being hung on his own gallows.

Applications

1. Ask if students ever told a story like this: "My dad's truck is the best."
2. Has anyone said something like this? "I always get 100% on my spelling tests."
3. Proud students want to be noticed by saying their grades loudly: "100%!"
4. Showing off by riding bike without holding onto the handlebar in front of your friends or visitors is pride. If you're too focused on showing off, you can wreck and hurt yourself. Pride is painful. Whether you wreck or not, pride is wrong.

Additional ideas

- Pride makes us hate instruction and reproof. We think we are right. We do not want to be told we are wrong.

  Proverbs 15:10—Correction is grievous unto him that forsaketh the way: and he that hateth reproof shall die.

  Proverbs 13:18—Poverty and shame shall be to him that refuseth instruction: but he that regardeth reproof shall be honoured.

- Proud people often have few true friends because others dislike their boasting or their attitudes.

- God hates pride.

  Proverbs 6:16, 17—These six things doth the LORD hate: yea, seven are an abomination unto him: a proud look, a lying tongue, and hands that shed innocent blood.

5

Planning Ahead

Theme

We must be faithful in many small choices in preparation for larger choices.

Items you will need

○ RushHour® logic game (A similar puzzle/logic game could work.)

Object lesson

Show the children the RushHour® game and explain the goal of getting the red car out. Why can't you just do that? What does moving the other cars have to do with getting the red car out?

Give the children a chance to help you try to get the red car out. Perhaps call for several volunteers if you do not have enough time for everyone to be involved.

○ Planning ahead is important.
○ Doing the right things today helps prepare us for the future.

- ○ Faithfulness in small details is needed to accomplish big goals.
- ○ Life has many choices that could move us toward our goal or away from it—it all depends on our choices.

Verses to consider

Proverbs 4:18—But the path of the just is as the shining light, that shineth more and more unto the perfect day.

Ecclesiastes 7:8—Better is the end of a thing than the beginning thereof: and the patient in spirit is better than the proud in spirit.

Philippians 3:13, 14—Brethren, I count not myself to have apprehended: but this one thing I do, forgetting those things which are behind, and reaching forth unto those things which are before, I press toward the mark for the prize of the high calling of God in Christ Jesus.

Matthew 25:21—His lord said unto him, Well done, thou good and faithful servant: thou hast been faithful over a few things, I will make thee ruler over many things: enter thou into the joy of thy lord.

Applications

1. Obedience today in small things prepares us to obey God in adult life.
2. School has many small things that prepare us for harder lessons.

○ We learn the letters and sounds before we can read.

○ We learn simple math facts so we can do harder math problems later.

○ We learn Bible memory today so we can use it later in life.

3. We do chores today to prepare us to do a job faithfully as an adult.

4. If we carefully plan ahead, we are better prepared for the future. Think of the ant gathering her food in the summer, knowing that winter is coming.

5. We develop lasting character today by sticking at our work, following directions, and promptly finishing our work.

Sin Is Dangerous

Theme

Playing with sin is like playing with fire.

Items you will need

- A candle
- A lighter
- A piece of paper

  Note: If the paper is used inside a building, have a metal container with a lid in case the paper needs to be extinguished. Great caution must be used to avoid an accidental fire. This lesson may work better in an outdoor setting.

Object lesson

Light the candle and let it burn where the children can see. Show them you can pass your finger through the flame quickly, but it won't hurt you.

Ask the children if a piece of paper would burn if it were put in the flame. Swipe the paper through the flame fast enough that it does not burn. Or hold the paper above the candle and ask students how close they think you can get before it will burn (practice in advance).

- ○ Sin is enticing and exciting, just like fire.
- ○ You can play with sin and sometimes seemingly control it, but sin always gets out of control.
- ○ Sin may seem bright, warm, and inviting at first, but it always destroys.

Verses to consider

Proverbs 6:27, 28—Can a man take fire in his bosom, and his clothes not be burned? Can one go upon hot coals, and his feet not be burned?

Judges 16:6-30—The story of Samson

Applications

1. Sin is always harmful.
2. Playing with sin pulls us closer and closer. We will want more of it.
   - ○ Disobeying rules might be thrilling, and we might get by for a while.
   - ○ Cheating or copying answers from others seems so much easier than figuring it out ourselves.
   - ○ Showing off to others is a lot of fun. We can get more and more attention, but it is wrong!
   - ○ Stealing (or any sin) becomes addictive. Thieves want more of the thrill or more "free" things.

    ○ Telling an untruth might cover up a wrong we did and keep us out of trouble temporarily, but our sin will eventually be discovered.

3. It is hard to stop the flame when it finally catches us.
4. There are eternal consequences for sin. Hell is a flame of punishment.

Additional ideas

1. Tell a personal story of a time when you played with fire (or something dangerous or sinful), and it got out of hand.
2. Tell a story about a fire you know of that was started by carelessness.
3. Research the Great Chicago Fire and tell how a small fire in one place spread quickly through the city.

7

Authority

Theme

Obedience and respect for authority protects us.

Items you will need

- An umbrella

Object lesson

Begin by asking what authority is and who the children's authorities are. Tell the children the umbrella represents our authorities. Open the umbrella and stand under it to illustrate being under an authority.

- When you obey, you are protected by that authority.
- If you disobey and rebel, you step out from under that protection.
- Authorities are placed over us to help us and protect us.
- Godly authorities want only what is for our good.

Verses to consider

Hebrews 13:17—Obey them that have the rule over you, and submit yourselves: for they watch for your souls, as they that must give account, that they may do it with joy, and not with grief: for that is unprofitable for you.

Ephesians 6:1-3—Children, obey your parents in the Lord: for this is right. Honour thy father and mother; (which is the first commandment with promise;) that it may be well with thee, and thou mayest live long on the earth.

Applications

1. Rules are to help us do what is right and what pleases God.
2. Godly parents and teachers are responsible to help us choose the good and right way.
3. Obeying their direction places us under their protection.
   - Our parents may have the rule that we may not go out around the barn while the silo is being filled. Or maybe it's a shop on our property that children must stay out of. They are protecting us from the dangerous machinery.
   - They might keep us from becoming a close friend to the neighbor. They are protecting us from bad influences—bad language, stories, movies, or smoking, for example.
   - At school we may not be allowed to cross the road if a ball goes across the road. The teachers are protecting us from being hit by a car.

○ Parents ask us to be prompt with our lessons and chores. They are protecting us from becoming lazy and careless.

○ Parents may have a rule against riding bike on the road in front of the house. They are protecting us from the danger of getting hit by a car.

○ Parents might tell young people what time to be home at night. They are protecting them from temptations.

Additional ideas

1. Jonah stepped out from under God's protection and was swallowed by a giant fish.

2. You could explain how all authorities on earth are under other authorities. But God is under no one. He is *sovereign*, which means He doesn't need to obey anyone above Him because there is no one above Him.

People Are Different

Theme

We should appreciate all the different people God made.

Items you will need

- Crayons of varying lengths, thicknesses, and colors
  - A brown crayon; a peach crayon
  - A broken crayon; a crayon with a frayed wrapper
  - A long, thin pencil crayon; a short, stubby crayon
  - Several crayons taped together in a row; two identical crayons
- Two identical pictures
  - One colored with only one color
  - One colored with many colors

Object lesson

Explain that the varying crayons illustrate different sorts of people. Some people are tall and slender (the pencil crayon), while others are short and plump (stubby crayon). Some people are crippled (broken crayon); some people are poor (crayon with ripped or frayed wrapper). Some people are twins (two identical crayons). Some people have dark skin (brown crayon); some have light skin (peach crayon). Some people have large families (several crayons taped together).

Show the two pictures you have colored: one with one color, the other in many different colors. This illustrates the value of every person making a contribution in life. We should appreciate every person God made. No one is the same, not even twins! Being different from each other adds color to our lives.

- The world is full of different kinds of people, yet we all came from Adam and Eve.
- People have different families, backgrounds, national-ities, and features, yet we're all just crayons—people!
- Personalities are different too.
- It is tempting to mock people who are not like us. We should remember we are mocking God when we mock others.

Verses to consider

2 Kings 2:23—And he went up from thence unto Bethel: and as he was going up by the way, there came forth little children out of the city, and mocked him, and said unto him, Go up, thou bald head; go up, thou bald head. *James 2:1-4*—My brethren, have not the faith of our Lord Jesus Christ, the Lord of glory, with respect of persons. For if there come unto your assembly a man with a gold ring, in goodly apparel, and there come in also a poor man in vile raiment; and ye have respect to him that weareth the gay clothing, and say unto him, Sit thou here in a good place; and say to the poor, Stand thou there, or sit here under my footstool: are ye not then partial in yourselves, and are become judges of evil thoughts?

Acts 10:34, 35—Then Peter opened his mouth, and said, Of a truth I perceive that God is no respecter of persons: but in every nation he that feareth him, and worketh righteousness, is accepted with him.

Colossians 3:25—But he that doeth wrong shall receive for the wrong which he hath done: and there is no respect of persons.

1 John 3:18—My little children, let us not love in word, neither in tongue; but in deed and in truth.

Applications

1. We must love and appreciate everyone around us.
2. We should never mock people whom we think are strange.
3. We should treat all people alike without favoritism or cliques.
4. Friends bring a lot of joy and blessings to our lives.
5. God designed the church to benefit from being made up of many different people.

Orderliness

Theme

God is a God of order and expects us to be orderly too.

Items you will need

- A desktop office organizer
- Office items to fill the organizer: paper clips, push pins, rubber bands, pens, and erasers, for example

Object lesson

You can do this in different ways. You can have the organizer in total disarray and ask a child to come up and help you organize it. Or you can have it neatly organized and pull some things out while you talk, then put them back in chaotic order.

As you work, you could share the verses to consider. Point out how organization is helpful to us and to others so we know what to expect or where to find something. Disorganization makes life more difficult.

You could discuss how creation is very orderly and shows us a picture of God's character. Consider the orderliness of the sun in its orbit and the stars in their constellations. Things God made are so orderly that scientists use the movement of the stars and planets to calculate time.

Verses to consider

1 Corinthians 14:33—For God is not the author of confusion, but of peace, as in all churches of the saints.

1 Corinthians 14:40—Let all things be done decently and in order.

Applications

1. We should be neat and orderly.
2. Orderliness helps us to be able to find our things.
3. We are known for how orderly (or not) we are; it is part of our reputation.
4. Orderliness is especially helpful when we are in a group setting like school. If everyone drops play equipment and jackets wherever they feel like, school becomes chaotic.
5. Orderliness helps us know what comes next: a schedule brings order to our day.
6. Orderliness at home is a blessing for the family. We should put away things when we are finished with them.

10

Slow to Speak

Theme

We should think before we speak—once spoken, words can never be taken back.

Items you will need

- A can of foam shaving cream
- A small dish
- A spoon

Object lesson

Begin by telling students that we should be careful what we say. Sometimes we blurt out something without thinking, and it hurts others or gets us into trouble. Perhaps we are angry or simply thoughtless or exaggerating to impress others.

Spray a pile of shaving cream into the dish to illustrate someone talking without thinking first. This could be an angry explosion or a hurtful comment or a big story that was exaggerated. We wish we could take it back.

Ask for a volunteer to come forward. Give him the spoon and ask him to put it all back into the can. This shows the impossibility of taking our words back.

Verses to consider

James 1:19—Wherefore, my beloved brethren, let every man be swift to hear, slow to speak, slow to wrath.

Proverbs 10:19—In the multitude of words there wanteth not sin: but he that refraineth his lips is wise.

Ecclesiastes 5:1, 2—Keep thy foot when thou goest to the house of God, and be more ready to hear, than to give the sacrifice of fools: for they consider not that they do evil. Be not rash with thy mouth, and let not thine heart be hasty to utter any thing before God: for God is in heaven, and thou upon earth: therefore let thy words be few.

Proverbs 17:27—He that hath knowledge spareth his words: and a man of understanding is of an excellent spirit.

Applications

1. We should be careful how we speak.
2. It is better to listen than to always be talking.
3. When we talk a lot, we often say some wrong things.
4. God hears what we say and He knows if it is good or bad.

5. When we say something we shouldn't, we need to apologize and ask forgiveness.

Additional ideas

1. Tell a story of a time when you said something you later wished you could take back.
2. Samson is an example of someone who told something he later regretted. He told the secret about his strength.

God's Greatness

Theme

God is greater than anything in the universe, yet He cares about small people.

Items you will need

- A globe
- Several balls to represent the moon, the planets, the sun, and other stars

Object lesson

Set the globe on a table close to your lectern to represent the world. Call on some children to hold balls to represent the moon, the planets, the sun, and some stars. Space them out as you have room. Have another child stand farthest away on a chair to represent God who is above the universe, yet He looks down on earth and sees man. How big a dot would you be if you were represented on this globe?

Point out how the student representing God's position cannot even read the names of the continents on the globe, but God is so great He can be above the universe, yet close to each one of us. He is above all the stars, yet He has named each one—how much better He knows each person!

Verses to consider

Psalm 8:3, 4—When I consider thy heavens, the work of thy fingers, the moon and the stars, which thou hast ordained; what is man, that thou art mindful of him? and the son of man, that thou visitest him?

Luke 12:6, 7—Are not five sparrows sold for two farthings, and not one of them is forgotten before God? But even the very hairs of your head are all numbered. Fear not therefore: ye are of more value than many sparrows.

Isaiah 66:1—Thus saith the Lord, The heaven is my throne, and the earth is my footstool: where is the house that ye build unto me? and where is the place of my rest?

Psalm 138:6—Though the Lord be high, yet hath he respect unto the lowly: but the proud he knoweth afar off.

Isaiah 57:15—For thus saith the high and lofty One that inhabiteth eternity, whose name is Holy; I dwell in the high and holy place, with him also that is of a contrite and humble spirit, to revive the spirit of the humble, and to revive the heart of the contrite ones.

Applications

1. We serve a mighty God, the Creator of the universe.
2. His power and greatness exceed anything we can imagine.
3. We do not need to be afraid. We can trust Him.
4. He sees what is going on around us—He is right here!

Additional ideas

1. How fast does God travel? God is omnipresent. So He is in Heaven and in the earth at the same time. He simply is everywhere!
2. How big is God? See Isaiah 40:12.

12

God's Chastening

Theme

Chastening and correction are for our good.

Items you will need

- An electric or manual pencil sharpener
- Several pencils to sharpen: a new one, a dull one, a broken one

Object lesson

In order for a pencil to be useful, it must be a sharp pencil. Show the dull pencil and say it can represent someone who is getting a bit careless with obedience. The broken pencil is an example of a person who is disrespectful and disobedient. The new pencil could represent a small child who is learning how to obey.

Ask the children if they know what chastening is. Explain that chastening is loving correction we receive when we disobey so we can learn to live right. One by one, "chasten" the pencils by sharpening them. Show how each pencil is now sharp and useful again. This is how we are after we've been corrected.

Also consider which pencil had the hardest time with chastening. The broken (rebellious) pencil had to have more sharpened away. The sharper we keep ourselves, the less we will need chastening.

- Everyone needs some correction at times. We tend to stray from the good and right way.
- Chastening is for our good if we accept it.
- God chastens His people when they do wrong because He loves them.
- Parents and teachers chasten children because they love them.

Verses to consider

Hebrews 12:11—Now no chastening for the present seemeth to be joyous, but grievous: nevertheless afterward it yieldeth the peaceable fruit of righteousness unto them which are exercised thereby.

Job 5:17—Behold, happy is the man whom God correcteth: therefore despise not thou the chastening of the Almighty.

Proverbs 15:10—Correction is grievous unto him that forsaketh the way: and he that hateth reproof shall die.

Proverbs 22:15—Foolishness is bound in the heart of a child; but the rod of correction shall drive it far from him.

Applications

1. We should learn to submit to correction or rebuke.
2. We must humbly listen to and obey our authorities—parents, teachers, and ministers.
3. We should decide to always do better when we are corrected instead of getting angry about it.
4. Submitting to correction will help us to please God as we grow up.
5. Chastening involves various aspects:
   - Reproofs or rebukes: When you are spoken to about what you did wrong and told that you must do better.
   - Restitution: We often are required to redo our work if we were sloppy or to repair something we damaged.
   - Apology: If we treated someone unkindly, we must apologize to them.
   - Punishment: Correction often involves losing a privilege for a time.
   - Discipline: Spankings are also used for chastening.

Additional ideas

1. Ask the older ones how they think God may chasten adults. (Not all negative things in life come from God, nor are they all chastening. Think of the story in John 9 of the man born blind.)

- ○ Through suffering or loss
- ○ By other authorities giving correction
- ○ By humiliation after making a wrong choice
- ○ By some special plans being interrupted or canceled

2. Anger and bitterness always lead to more sin and more need for chastening.

A Soft Answer

Theme

A soft answer will turn away wrath.

Items you will need

- A quart jar filled one-third with white vinegar
- Baking soda
- A large dishpan

Object lesson

Set the jar in the dishpan. Tell students the jar represents someone who is upset and angry. Ask them what happens when you irritate someone who is angry.

Spoon in some baking soda and watch the vinegar react and foam. This demonstrates how angry words only stir up more anger.

Verses to consider

Proverbs 15:1—A soft answer turneth away wrath: but grievous words stir up anger.

Judges 8:1-3—Consider how Gideon's soft answer turned away wrath.

1 Samuel 25—Consider Nabal's harsh response to David's servants and then Abigail's wise entreaty.

Proverbs 25:15—By long forbearing is a prince persuaded, and a soft tongue breaketh the bone.

Matthew 5:44—But I say unto you, Love your enemies, bless them that curse you, do good to them that hate you, and pray for them which despitefully use you, and persecute you.

Applications

1. Being kind to angry people helps them calm down.

2. We are tempted to use harsh words when people are upset at us, but that only makes the problem worse.

3. Kindness is always the right choice in bad situations. People may still be upset, but we won't be responsible for making it worse.

4. A kind deed may appease an angry person.
   - A gift to an enemy may soften his heart.
   - Being helpful when someone needs a hand can speak to a hard-hearted person.
   - Being friendly and visiting even if they act unfriendly to us is kind.

5. Wrong responses make matters worse.
   - Gossiping to others about our enemy will hurt and stir up more anger.
   - Mocking an angry person will cause more strife.
   - Sharp words and mean actions will hurt deeply.

Additional ideas

1. Tell a story from your own experience where someone was made even angrier by angry words. Then
   contrast with a story of soft words turning away
   anger.
2. Look at the story of Naaman (2 Kings 5). A servant
   with soft words of wisdom spoke to angry Naaman
   and helped him reconsider his choices.

14

Proper Priorities

Theme

We must do the important things of life first in order to have success.

Items you will need

- A wide-mouth gallon jar
- Several apples
- A bag of sugar or rice (dry sand could work)
  Note: Practice ahead of time to determine the amount you need.
- A dishpan

Object lesson

The apples illustrate the important things of life: reading the Bible, praying, doing our chores, doing our school-work, for example. The sugar or rice illustrates the lesser things of life, maybe even the fun things: going fishing, riding bike, or playing doll, for example. Put the apples in the jar first and then fill it up with the sugar or rice. Everything fits!

Now dump it all out in a dishpan and try again. Put the sugar or rice in first and see if you can get all the apples in. You cannot. This illustrates that if you put the important things in life first, the rest can be filled up with the lesser things; but if you try to have your fun first, you'll miss the important things.

Verses to consider

Matthew 6:33—But seek ye first the kingdom of God, and his righteousness; and all these things shall be added unto you.

1 Kings 3:5-13—Solomon asks for wisdom first and gets riches also.

Mark 12:29-31—And Jesus answered him, The first of all the commandments is, Hear, O Israel; The Lord our God is one Lord: and thou shalt love the Lord thy God with all thy heart, and with all thy soul, and with all thy mind, and with all thy strength: this is the first commandment. And the second is like, namely this, Thou shalt love thy neighbour as thyself. There is none other commandment greater than these.

Proverbs 4:7—Wisdom is the principal thing; therefore get wisdom: and with all thy getting get understanding.

Luke 10:42—But one thing is needful: and Mary hath chosen that good part, which shall not be taken away from her.

Applications

1. God wants us to put Him first in our lives.
2. We should take time to read our Bibles, pray, and go to church.
3. Learning obedience, love, humility, and good manners as children is important.
4. Helping others is another important part of doing God's work.
5. Doing our homework for school should be done before we play.
6. After the important things are done, we can enjoy some leisure time. In fact, we enjoy it more because we know we have finished the important things.

Additional ideas

1. The most important thing in life is to make our choice to follow Jesus. Personal salvation should never be put off for some earthly pleasure.
2. Many Christian service opportunities are only available for a short time. For example, young people have opportunities that older ones don't. We should take advantage of the opportunities we have.

15

Giving in Secret

Theme

We should give willingly and not for show.

Items you will need

- A large amount of coins
- A metal dishpan

Object lesson

Read the story about the rich men and the poor widow in Mark 12:41-44. Take a handful of money and proudly throw it into the dishpan to make a lot of noise. People would turn and look at a rich person putting in much money. Repeat this a few times; then take two small coins and gently drop them in to illustrate the widow putting in two mites.

Jesus noticed the poor widow because of her humble and selfless attitude. He was critical of those who gave much because they were trying to get people to look at them.

Verses to consider

Matthew 6:2, 3—Therefore when thou doest thine alms, do not sound a trumpet before thee, as the hypocrites do in the synagogues and in the streets, that they may have glory of men. Verily I say unto you, They have their reward. But when thou doest alms, let not thy left hand know what thy right hand doeth.

2 Corinthians 9:7—Every man according as he purposeth in his heart, so let him give; not grudgingly, or of necessity: for God loveth a cheerful giver.

Applications

1. God notices our giving.
2. God wants us to give cheerfully.
3. God does not want us to show off with our giving.
4. If we get attention with our giving, we have our reward today. God wants us to do it in secret, and He will reward us for it. We shouldn't talk about how much we gave.
5. God owns the universe. He blesses us with money that we can use to bless the church, missions, and other people who need help.

Additional ideas

1. You could contrast giving grudgingly and giving cheerfully.
2. Talk about places that depend on our giving—missions, schools, churches.

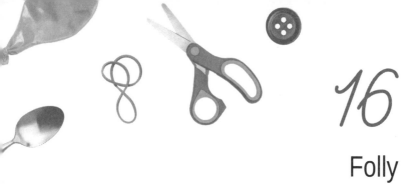

16

Folly

Theme

A little folly brings much trouble.

Items you will need

○ A fly tape or flytrap full of dead flies

○ A cup of yogurt

Object lesson

Begin by explaining what a good reputation is. Then explain what folly or foolishness is.

Ask the children if any of them ever use lotion. Ask them what they think would happen if there were dead flies in their lotion bottle. That's how a little folly is to someone's good reputation.

Ask how many of them like yogurt. Take the cup of yogurt and put a dead fly, or several, in it and stir it up. Would they eat it now? It is only one small bad thing in a whole cup of good yogurt. Does it really matter? This is how a little folly is to someone's good name. One little wrong can spoil a lot.

Verses to consider

Ecclesiastes 10:1—Dead flies cause the ointment of the apothecary to send forth a stinking savour: so doth a little folly him that is in reputation for wisdom and honour.

1 Samuel 25:25—Let not my lord, I pray thee, regard this man of Belial, even Nabal: for as his name is, so is he; Nabal is his name, and folly is with him: but I thine handmaid saw not the young men of my lord, whom thou didst send.

Proverbs 15:21—Folly is joy to him that is destitute of wisdom: but a man of understanding walketh uprightly.

Ecclesiastes 2:13—Then I saw that wisdom excelleth folly, as far as light excelleth darkness.

Applications

Folly is a lack of good sense, understanding, or foresight. A similar word is *foolishness*. Consider some examples of folly.

1. A joke that belittles or embarrasses someone
2. An action that ends with something broken, lost, or destroyed
3. Showing off, acting smart, or boasting

Additional ideas

1. Tell a story of a time when a little folly ended up causing a big problem.

A Creation Lesson:
A Chick Is Hatched

Theme

God's designs in creation are marvelous.

Items you will need

○ A chicken egg or two
○ A new chick, if possible
○ Dishes for the white and yolk, if you choose

Object lesson

Hold up the egg as you talk to let the children see it. You could crack an egg open to show the white and yolk inside as you come to those parts. Save the live chick as a surprise ending.

Have you ever wondered what a chick experiences as he grows in an egg? Two important tubes connect a chick to the food supply (the yoke) and the outside oxygen source. Over ten thousand microscopic holes in the shell allow oxygen to come in and carbon dioxide to go out. The shell has a coating to keep dust out of the holes.

The little chick is safely held in the center of the egg by two strong bungee-like cords connected to the opposite ends of the shell. It is also protected by a dense liquid, the white, which is full of protein and a powerful enzyme known as *lysozyme*. This enzyme kills bacteria, protecting the chick from infection.

A few days before hatching, the chick grows a special tool called an egg tooth on the tip of its beak. It uses this tool to open a special air sack to give it about six hours of oxygen, which it needs before chiseling its way out of the shell.

The day before the chick hatches, it swallows the remaining food pack, the yolk. This gives it about three days of food and water to live on. With this oxygen and food giving it energy, the chick cracks open its shell and bursts forth into life in this world. What a marvelous design of an all-wise Creator God!

Verses to consider

Psalm 147:9—He giveth to the beast his food, and to the young ravens which cry.

Luke 12:6—Are not five sparrows sold for two farthings, and not one of them is forgotten before God?

Psalm 143:5—I remember the days of old; I meditate on all thy works; I muse on the work of thy hands.

Applications

1. God is wise and knows what's best for us. He is our Creator!
2. God will take care of us. He never forgets his creation.
3. We can trust God for strength for duties each day. He knows how much each of us can take.
4. We should respect animal life that God so wonderfully made.

Additional ideas

1. You could break open a fertilized egg and see if anyone can see anything like a chick inside.
2. Eggshells cut in half are very strong and will hold up a stack of books. You have to punch a hole and empty the inside out. Take tape and circle the middle of the shell where you will cut. Cut as straight as possible and leave the tape on. (The tape keeps the shell from crumbling when you cut it. If you try to remove it, you will break the shell.)

   Put four half shells on a towel. Stack books on top until they break. Today's dome-shaped architectural designs have tremendous strength despite all the open space inside.

Forgiveness

Theme

We need forgiveness when we do wrong.

Items you will need

- ○ Red food coloring
- ○ Two quart jars, half-filled with water
- ○ A long spoon
- ○ Liquid bleach

Object lesson

Tell the children that the jars of water represent our hearts and the food coloring represents sin (when we disobey or do wrong). Put two drops of food coloring in each jar to represent sin stains in the two hearts. Stir it around and notice that both hearts are full of sin; they are guilty! You can refer to Romans 3:23, "For all have sinned, and come short of the glory of God." Ask the children if they could clean the food coloring out of the water.

Tell them when we sin, we must be sorry, tell our parents, and ask God for forgiveness. The bleach represents

God's forgiveness. Pour about a tablespoon of bleach into one of the jars to "cleanse the sin away." You must stir it and give it a little time to clear up the coloring. God is able to clean our hearts from sin. (Practice beforehand to know how long it takes for the type of bleach and food coloring you have.)

By having one jar still full of sin (unbleached), you can see the contrast. You could talk about how the guilty heart feels compared to the heart that is forgiven and free. You can go on with your lesson and come back to check on the forgiven "man" at the end. Are there any traces of sin in his life?

Verses to consider

1 John 1:9—If we confess our sins, he is faithful and just to forgive us our sins, and to cleanse us from all unrighteousness.

Psalm 51:2—Wash me throughly from mine iniquity, and cleanse me from my sin.

Proverbs 28:13—He that covereth his sins shall not prosper: but whoso confesseth and forsaketh them shall have mercy.

Ephesians 1:7—In whom we have redemption through his blood, the forgiveness of sins, according to the riches of his grace.

Applications

1. Forgiveness means that the wrong action is cleared up. We are free.
2. For small children, forgiveness comes by telling their parents what they did wrong. Parents correct or punish, and then it is forgiven.
3. For older ones, we confess it to God, and He forgives us and sets us free.
4. Confession is the key; it means to tell on myself, either to God or to my parents.
5. Covering sin makes it worse; it makes us miserable.

Additional ideas

1. Look at the story of Achan in Joshua 7 and how he covered up his sin. He did not get it cleansed.
2. Consider the story of Zacchaeus in Luke 19. He sought to see Jesus, confessed his sin, and committed himself to restitution.

The Floating Ax-Head

Theme

God is able to solve our problems.

Items you will need

- A large clear plastic tub filled with water
- An ax-head or other metal tool
- A large stick and a small stick

Object lesson

Look at the story in 2 Kings 6 where Elisha made the ax-head swim. Drop the ax-head into the water to illustrate the problem. Then ask someone to come up and follow your instructions to retrieve this ax-head.

Have the child try throwing the small stick into the water; when that doesn't work, tell him to try poking it in or stirring the water. See if they can find any way to make the ax-head swim. Could another person do it better? Would another stick, a bigger one, do better?

It was God's power, not Elisha or the stick, that made the ax-head swim.

What if the young men had not invited Elisha along? What would they have done to get this ax-head? Do you think they would ever have found it again?

Verses to consider

Philippians 4:19—But my God shall supply all your need according to his riches in glory by Christ Jesus.

1 Peter 5:7—Casting all your care upon him; for he careth for you.

Matthew 19:26—But Jesus beheld them, and said unto them, With men this is impossible; but with God all things are possible.

Applications

1. God wants to help us with our problems. He is all-powerful. Nothing is too hard for God.
2. We should ask God each day to go with us to help us, protect us, and bless our work.
3. We should pray for God's help when we are facing a problem. Nothing is too large or too small for God.
4. The man who lost the ax-head told the problem to Elisha. We should tell our problems to our parents or adults who can help us.
5. We can trust God for all our needs in life. He often does not give us exactly what we think we need, but He will help us find a way.

6. We should have our parents close by to help us if something bad happens to us. We should not wander off without parents knowing where we are going.

Additional ideas

1. Tell a story of a time when you had a problem, you prayed about it, and God answered.
2. You can use the part of working together in 2 Kings 6 to teach teamwork. You can point out that God blesses us when we work together.

20

The Conscience:
Our E.W.S.

Theme

God gave us each a conscience.

Items you will need

- Chalkboard or whiteboard
- A household battery-operated fire alarm
- Matches and/or a candle

Object lesson

Write the letters E.W.S. on the board in large letters. Ask the children to guess what the letters stand for. It stands for Early Warning System. Our conscience is our early warning system. It warns us when we are about to make a bad choice.

Light the match or candle and use it to set off the fire alarm (practice in advance). Point out that the alarm rings early, long before the room is filled with smoke. So it is with our conscience: it warns us long before we make big bad choices.

Using the match or candle, set off the alarm again. Let it ring while you try to talk. It hurts our ears and drowns out our conversation. We must tend to this problem. It is like a screaming conscience.

Verses to consider

Proverbs 20:27—The spirit of man is the candle of the Lord, searching all the inward parts of the belly.

1 Timothy 1:5—Now the end of the commandment is charity out of a pure heart, and of a good conscience, and of faith unfeigned.

Acts 24:16—And herein do I exercise myself, to have always a conscience void of offence toward God, and toward men.

John 8:9—And they which heard it, being convicted by their own conscience, went out one by one, beginning at the eldest, even unto the last: and Jesus was left alone, and the woman standing in the midst.

1 Timothy 4:2—Speaking lies in hypocrisy; having their conscience seared with a hot iron.

Titus 1:15—Unto the pure all things are pure: but unto them that are defiled and unbelieving is nothing pure; but even their mind and conscience is defiled.

Applications

1. God has given us a conscience that warns us early when we do wrong.
2. The conscience is an inner stirring, an uncomfortable feeling. Our heart gets scared; it beats faster; we feel guilty and bad.
3. A good conscience warns us when we are thinking of doing wrong so we can stop and choose to do right.
4. Our parents teach us right and wrong to shape our conscience.
5. The Bible teaches us right and wrong to teach our conscience.
6. If we ignore our conscience, it will get weaker. If we choose rebellion, our conscience will not work as well.

Additional ideas

1. Tell a story of a time when your conscience rang loud and clear and how you respond to it.
2. Genesis 42:21 shows the consciences of Joseph's brothers still bothering them after many years.

21

Helping Each Other

Theme

We need the help of our friends.

Items you will need

- ○ Four sticks, each about three feet long
- ○ Four pieces of thin rope or strong string
- ○ Two candy bars
- ○ Optional: Consider having enough candy bars for the whole class.

Object lesson

Ask for two volunteers. Fasten the sticks to their arms so they cannot bend their elbows. Be careful not to tie the string too tightly. Give each volunteer a candy bar and tell them to enjoy it. They cannot get it into their mouths without bending their elbows.

Keep encouraging them to eat the candy bars. Give them time to think about how they could solve their problem. If they don't think of it themselves, suggest that they can help each other get the candy to their mouths.

Explain that many things in life we cannot do on our own. We need others to help us. If we are too proud to ask for help, we will miss out on many good things. But when we all work together, we will be better off.

Verses to consider

Ecclesiastes 4:9, 10—Two are better than one; because they have a good reward for their labour. For if they fall, the one will lift up his fellow: but woe to him that is alone when he falleth; for he hath not another to help him up.

Proverbs 17:17—A friend loveth at all times, and a brother is born for adversity.

Proverbs 18:24—A man that hath friends must shew himself friendly: and there is a friend that sticketh closer than a brother.

Applications

1. We need each other especially in difficult times. Sometimes we cannot do for ourselves what we need—others must help us or do it for us.
   - We might break a leg and need medical help.
   - We may need help to put a bicycle chain back on.
   - We may need help to lift something heavy.
2. We should be quick to help others, and they will be more likely to help us. Remember the Golden Rule.
3. We can overcome obstacles by working together.
   - Picking peas goes much faster with everyone helping.

o Cleaning up after meals works best if everyone does their part.

o Games go best if everyone on a team takes part to help win.

Additional ideas

1. Tell a story of a time when you or someone you know needed help in an emergency.

2. Acts 9:1-19 tells how Saul needed someone to lead him while he was blind. He needed Ananias to pray for him.

3. An alternate object lesson on this theme is to bring two toy building blocks and a container such as an empty ice-cream bucket or large bowl. Set the three objects on a table. Ask two students to try to each get a block into the bucket before the other student. They are allowed to touch the block with only one finger. They may not move or touch the bucket.

Students may push the block around trying to imagine how to lift it into the bucket. The secret is for them to cooperate and push their blocks together. By pushing the blocks against each other, the students can carefully lift together until they can drop both blocks into the container.

Most younger students will not be able to figure this out without help. Ask for older volunteers next to see if they can discover the secret.

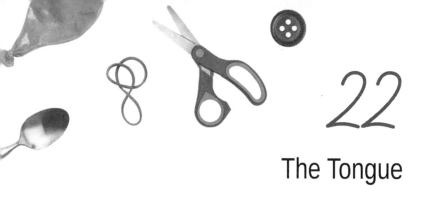

22

The Tongue

Theme

We must understand the power of the tongue and how to use it for good.

Items you will need

- One picture with small details colored neatly
- One picture with wrong color choices colored sloppily
- Optional: Have photocopied pictures to hand out for the students to color at home.

Object lesson

Introduce the idea of how important the tongue is by asking everyone to hold their tongues against the roof of their mouths while saying, "Good morning!" Notice how handicapped we are without our tongues to speak.

Show them the picture with small details colored carefully. Explain how we must choose the right words (the right colors) and stay within God's boundaries for our speech (the lines). Point out the small details done well and liken that to small specific encouragements or compliments you can give to someone today. While they don't seem great, they are small important contributions to the picture of life.

Then switch to the sloppy picture with wrong colors and scribbles outside the lines. Point out how ugly this picture is. No one wants this picture. This is a person who runs his mouth without carefully choosing his words. He doesn't know the boundaries of decency or of right and wrong. He tells bad stories, talks when others wish he would listen, and is rude. He gossips about others to try to make his picture look better and theirs look worse. No one enjoys someone like this.

Which picture will you choose to color today? (Hand out pictures for the students if you chose to bring them.)

Verses to consider

James 3:1-13—Verses about the tongue.

*Proverbs 10:20—*The tongue of the just is as choice silver: the heart of the wicked is little worth.

*Proverbs 15:2—*The tongue of the wise useth knowledge aright: but the mouth of fools poureth out foolishness.

*Proverbs 18:21—*Death and life are in the power of the tongue: and they that love it shall eat the fruit thereof.

Applications

1. Kind words bless people and make the day much nicer for everyone.

2. Our words should show consideration and love for others.

3. Honest speech makes a beautiful picture in our lives. Parents, teachers, and friends enjoy people who are honest. Dishonesty ruins our lives and reputations.

4. Our friends will not appreciate our selfish and proud speech.

5. Words of encouragement and cheer to someone who is sad or hurting make them happy. Most importantly, God blesses us when we care for hurting people.

Additional ideas

1. Tell a story of someone who blessed your life with encouraging words at a critical time.

2. Use Ananias and Sapphira as examples of dishonesty and its high cost (Acts 5).

3. Use the story of the unkind mockery toward Elisha (2 Kings 2).

23

God's Good Gifts

Theme

God loves to give us good gifts when we pray.

Items you will need

- A small stone
- A toy snake
- Optional: A small table to pretend it's mealtime

Object lesson

Arrange with two children beforehand to come and have one ask you for bread and the other for a fish. When one asks for bread, give him the stone. When the next one asks for a fish, pull out the toy snake for him.

Explain that God loves us, and He loves to give us good gifts. Ask the class to list some of the good gifts they've been given. Point out to them that all good and perfect gifts come from God. We could have nothing without Him.

Ask them if their parents always give them everything they ask for. Do they always get as much candy as they want? Does that mean their parents don't love them? No, it is because our parents know what's best for us that they choose not to always give us what we ask for.

Ask them if God always gives them what they pray for. What does that tell us about God? God knows everything about everyone. He knows what's best for us. He chooses to give us what we need, what's best for us, even if it may seem to hurt us in the moment. God loves to give us what we need.

Verses to consider

Luke 11:9-13—This is the passage from which the object lesson is taken.

James 1:17—Every good gift and every perfect gift is from above, and cometh down from the Father of lights, with whom is no variableness, neither shadow of turning.

Applications

1. God loves to hear our requests in prayer and to give us good gifts.
2. We should ask God when we need His help.
3. God wants to hear our requests, even if they are small.
4. God doesn't always give us what we want, but He will always do what is best for us.
5. We should share good gifts with others when they are in need.

Additional ideas

Consider the following gifts God gave:

1. God answered Hannah's prayer for a baby (1 Samuel 1).

2. Peter prayed and Dorcas was raised to life again (Acts 9:36-43).

3. Elijah prayed for rain and God answered (1 Kings 18:41-46; James 5:17, 18).

24

Hypocrisy

Theme

To understand what it means to be a hypocrite and how God hates hypocrisy.

Items you will need

- A large candy bar
- Two pieces of wood the shape and size of the candy bar

Object lesson

Advance preparation: Purchase a large Hershey's candy bar and carefully remove the candy, keeping the wrapper intact. Make a piece of wood the size of the candy bar. On the back of the wood write the word *Hypocrite* and wrap it in the candy wrapper. Make another piece of wood that is similar in size but not wrapped up nice. Put both items in a bag.

Begin your presentation by asking two students to come up and choose something they would like out of the bag. Usually the fake candy bar gets picked first. Ask the student with the fake candy bar to open his first.

Explain that the candy bar was not what it looked like on the outside. It was hypocritical. Hypocrisy is living a lie. It is pretending to be something we are not. Sometimes this is called being two-faced. We may pretend to be friends with John, but we make fun of him when we're with our other friends. We may act nice at school, but we may be grouchy and whiny or disobedient at home.

Jesus spoke very harshly against hypocrites. God wants us to be true and to live right all the time, even when others can't see. He is far more disappointed in hypocrites than we are with a fake candy bar.

Verses to consider

Job 8:13—So are the paths of all that forget God; and the hypocrite's hope shall perish.

Job 13:16—He also shall be my salvation: for an hypocrite shall not come before him.

Job 15:34—For the congregation of hypocrites shall be desolate, and fire shall consume the tabernacles of bribery.

Matthew 23:27, 28—Woe unto you, scribes and Pharisees, hypocrites! for ye are like unto whited sepulchres, which indeed appear beautiful outward, but are within full of dead men's bones, and of all uncleanness. Even so ye also outwardly appear righteous unto men, but within ye are full of hypocrisy and iniquity.

Applications

1. Hypocrisy is acting a lie, pretending to be something we are not.
2. God hates hypocrisy.
3. Hypocrites eventually get found out. Their sin gets exposed.

Additional ideas

1. Tell the story of the Gibeonites and their hypocrisy (Joshua 9).
2. Discuss why Jesus said that the Pharisees were hypocrites (Matthew 23).

Relating to Friends

Theme

We should treat others with kindness and respect.

Items you will need

- Flowers in a vase

Object lesson

Explain that a group of friends who get along are like this vase of flowers, beautiful and blessed. Then start talking about what happens when someone is hurtful to their friends (you could ask for ideas from the children).

As you describe hurtful things we can do to each other, begin plucking petals from the flowers. Following are some ideas:

- Unkind words and gossip destroy friendships.
- Refusing to accept when you are caught in a game ruins friendships and spoils the game.
- Laughing at someone who is poor or someone who gets a bad grade is unkind.
- Whispering secrets can make someone else feel left out.

○ Playing with just a few of your friends and ignoring other children is unkind.

Ask for a volunteer to put these friends back together by putting all the petals back on the flowers. It is impossible. The flower will take a long time to grow back; it may not come back until next year! When we destroy friendships, they can be ruined for a long time.

We know by God's grace friendships can be restored again, but it does not happen overnight. We must take great care with our friendships, even greater care than we take with a delicate flower.

Verses to consider

Proverbs 17:17—A friend loveth at all times, and a brother is born for adversity.

Proverbs 18:24—A man that hath friends must shew himself friendly: and there is a friend that sticketh closer than a brother.

Ephesians 4:32—And be ye kind one to another, tender-hearted, forgiving one another, even as God for Christ's sake hath forgiven you.

Applications

1. God wants us to be kind and friendly to all people.
2. When we are kind to others, they often return that kindness to us.
3. To have lots of friends, we each must be a friendly person.

4. If we are a selfish, proud, and hurtful person, we will lose our friends.

Additional ideas

1. Tell a story from your childhood when a friend was not so friendly and hurt you.
2. Dorcas was a kind friend who helped many people and they loved her (Acts 9:36-43).
3. Jonathan was a good friend of David; he went to him in the woods and encouraged him (1 Samuel 23:15-18).

26

Appreciating Others' Talents

Theme

We should consider the differing abilities of each person and notice how God's kingdom and our communities need different talents.

Items you will need

- Tape measure
- Square
- Hammer
- Saw
- Carpenter pencil

Object lesson

Display the tools one at a time and discuss how each one is used. What jobs can each one perform that the others cannot possibly do? Talk about their usefulness even though they are so different.

So how many tools does a man need to do his work? And if he had only one or two, could he do his job? (You could use mechanic tools as the objects instead of carpenter tools if you prefer.)

Verses to consider

Ephesians 4:11, 12—And he gave some, apostles; and some, prophets; and some, evangelists; and some, pastors and teachers; for the perfecting of the saints, for the work of the ministry, for the edifying of the body of Christ.
1 Corinthians 12—Teaches the concept of many members, one body.

Applications

1. God gives each person their abilities to be used for His glory and purposes.
2. The church needs a variety of workers and talents.
3. Our communities need different skills.
4. Some skills are more native to us, and some we must discover and develop.
5. Every person has something to contribute to the church and society.

Additional ideas

1. You could also ask students to list different kinds of jobs: mechanic, carpenter, plumber, truck driver, farmer, cashier, baker, seamstress, and more. Use those occupations to illustrate this same diversity in your community. Maybe you have this diversity in your congregation.

The Snare of Sin

Theme

Sin captures people and eventually destroys them.

Items you will need

- Various animal traps and snares

Object lesson

Set a few traps on a table. Demonstrate how the traps work; explain what animals they are for and what bait they use, if any. Explain how a trapper hides his trap in dirt or under leaves and places bait close by to lure the animal in to step in his trap. The goal is to conceal the trap and reveal the luscious bait. Even wary foxes fall for a properly set trap and bait.

Explain how the devil sets traps for us to tempt us to go against God. Sometimes the bait looks delicious, just like when Eve saw the forbidden fruit in the Garden of Eden. If we take the bait, we will be caught in sin and will suffer for our choices.

But God can deliver us from the traps of the devil. His

light of truth in the Bible and from our parents and church leaders can show us where traps are hidden so we can avoid them. We do not have get caught in sin.

Verses to consider

Psalm 91:3—Surely he shall deliver thee from the snare of the fowler, and from the noisome pestilence.

Psalm 119:110—The wicked have laid a snare for me: yet I erred not from thy precepts.

Proverbs 7:23—Till a dart strike through his liver; as a bird hasteth to the snare, and knoweth not that it is for his life.

2 Timothy 2:26—And that they may recover themselves out of the snare of the devil, who are taken captive by him at his will.

Applications

1. Temptations are like a snare set to catch us.
   - Cheating promises better grades.
   - Boasting and stretching stories promises that people will be impressed with us.
   - Stealing promises good things for us without a cost.
   - Disobedience promises happiness.

These promises are false. They are snares that bring only pain and eventually death.

2. Satan tries to disguise sin and make it look good and rewarding.
3. Evil people sometimes try to get us to go along with them in their sin.

Additional ideas

1. Tell the story of a man of God caught in a snare of a lying prophet (1 Kings 13).
2. Find a newspaper article of a criminal who was caught in sin and is now in jail. Share how Satan's snares take people further into sin.

28

Procrastination

Theme

We need to learn how to be prompt with our responses and assignments.

Items you will need

○ Yourself—late!

Object lesson

You can be the object for this lesson. Ahead of time, arrange with those in charge that you will arrive late. Rush in at the last minute, after they have waited past the starting time. Leave your notes or Bible in the back or outside, and then you can rush back to get them. This all illustrates what happens when we procrastinate, and at the last minute we try to quickly pull it together.

God expects us to be diligent. Procrastination (put off until later what should be done now) is delayed obedience—and delayed obedience is usually disobedience. Children who acquire the bad habit of procrastination can suffer from it for years.

God expects us to be caring and responsible. When we procrastinate, we are being selfish. Procrastination causes problems and frustrations for other people. God expects us to be honest and keep our word. Procrastination often causes us to be late for our commitments or to miss them altogether.

Verses to consider

Matthew 25:10—And while they went to buy, the bridegroom came; and they that were ready went in with him to the marriage: and the door was shut.

Luke 9:62—And Jesus said unto him, No man, having put his hand to the plough, and looking back, is fit for the kingdom of God.

Ecclesiastes 9:10—Whatsoever thy hand findeth to do, do it with thy might; for there is no work, nor device, nor knowledge, nor wisdom, in the grave, whither thou goest.

Romans 12:11—Not slothful in business; fervent in spirit; serving the Lord.

Colossians 3:23—And whatsoever ye do, do it heartily, as to the Lord, and not unto men.

Applications

1. It is important to promptly do what we know we must do.
2. Putting things off usually causes extra work and frustration.

3. A diligent worker gets an early start and finishes on time.

Additional ideas

1. Tell a story about a time when procrastination cost you or someone you know.
2. Consider Lot and his family taking too long to get out of Sodom. The angels had to physically pull them out of Sodom (Genesis 19).

The Importance of Starting Right

Theme

If we want to end up right, we must start out right.

Items you will need

○ A suit coat or other coat with large buttons (a large shirt could also work)

Object lesson

You will need to wear your suit for this lesson. When you get up front, start buttoning your coat at the bottom, but start buttoning one hole off from the correct way. As you continue to button, it will become clear that something isn't right.

Unbutton it and try again, but start off wrong again. Talk about the importance of starting right to end up right. Then button your coat correctly and show how smoothly it goes.

Verses to consider

Lamentations 3:27—It is good for a man that he bear the yoke in his youth.

1 Peter 4:17—For the time is come that judgment must begin at the house of God: and if it first begin at us, what shall the end be of them that obey not the gospel of God?

Applications

1. Starting right and continuing right is important for a good ending.
2. Youth is a time to learn to live for God.
3. We should ponder the result of our choices and not consider only the present.

Additional ideas

1. Balaam wanted to end up right but wasn't willing to live right. "Who can count the dust of Jacob, and the number of the fourth part of Israel? Let me die the death of the righteous, and let my last end be like his!" (Numbers 23:10).
2. Think about Noah not putting off building the ark. What if he would have waited fifty years then had to really hurry to get it done?

When Provoked

Theme

We should respond softly or not at all when provoked.

Items you will need

- A bed sheet
- An egg

Object lesson

Have two older children hold the sheet up at a bit more than a 45 degree angle with a curl at the bottom. Bring an egg along and have another child hurl the egg into the sheet. (Practice this at home to make sure your setup works as intended.) You cannot break the egg by hitting the sheet. The curl at the bottom catches the egg after it hits the sheet.

People will hurl provoking words and actions at us, but we do not need to be offended. Ask the students what would happen if the egg were thrown at a wall. Our response will make the difference. If we are soft like the sheet, we will not be offended. But if we are hard like the wall, we will be easily offended when others throw unkind things our way.

Verses to consider

Proverbs 15:1—A soft answer turneth away wrath: but grievous words stir up anger.

1 Corinthians 13:5—Doth not behave itself unseemly, seeketh not her own, is not easily provoked, thinketh no evil.

Ephesians 4:2—With all lowliness and meekness, with longsuffering, forbearing one another in love.

Applications

1. We should not be easily provoked when others mistreat us.
2. Love will help us to patiently accept wrong treatment without getting upset.
3. God wants us to learn to forbear and be long-suffering.

Additional ideas

1. Look at the example of Stephen when his enemies gnashed their teeth (Acts 7:54-60).
2. Jesus is an example of not getting provoked when they took Him to crucify Him (Luke 22:47-54).

31

What's in Your Heart?

Theme

We should fill our hearts with good things.

Items you will need

○ Kitchen scraps or rotten food
○ A beautiful bowl filled with fresh fruit

Object lesson

The question is simple: Is your heart a slop bucket? Or is it a bowl of the fruit of the Spirit? Our hearts always have something in them. We have thoughts and attitudes about others, about our authorities, and about our duties. We imagine and dream of things we would like to do. We hear stories and jokes and repeat them to others.

What does God see when He looks into our hearts? What do others see in us when they relate to us? Do kindness, love, and humility come from our lips and actions? Do we only tell clean stories and jokes?

Verses to consider

Galatians 5:22, 23—But the fruit of the Spirit is love, joy, peace, longsuffering, gentleness, goodness, faith, meekness, temperance: against such there is no law.

Matthew 12:34, 35—O generation of vipers, how can ye, being evil, speak good things? for out of the abundance of the heart the mouth speaketh. A good man out of the good treasure of the heart bringeth forth good things: and an evil man out of the evil treasure bringeth forth evil things.

Proverbs 4:23—Keep thy heart with all diligence; for out of it are the issues of life.

Applications

1. We must only put good things into our hearts.
2. What we think about will come out in our actions and words.
3. A pure heart will make a pure life.
4. Others can tell what is in your heart by looking at your life.

Additional ideas

1. Simon had a heart problem. "Thou hast neither part nor lot in this matter: for thy heart is not right in the sight of God" (Acts 8:21).

2. The bowl of good fruit could also represent a class-room of good students. When everyone does what is right, it is beautiful. But at times someone disobeys or is unkind, and that is like pouring slop into the good bowl. It makes trouble for everyone.

32

The Bible Is Our Guide

Theme

The Bible is for our instruction and direction.

Items you will need

- A car manual
- A road map or atlas
- A driver's manual
- A dictionary
- A lamp or lantern
- A jar of honey

Object lesson

Spread the objects on a table or hold them up one by one. Have the children first identify each object, and then have them try to tell you how each one is like the Bible.

Several objects can illustrate the Bible. (1) Motor manuals from a shop instruct us how to fix things. The Bible instructs us how to fix our hearts. (2) A road map shows us how to get to our destination. The Bible shows us how to get to Heaven to be with God. (3) A driver's manual tells us the rules of the road and how to safely drive. The Bible tells us the laws of God and how to stay on the right road. (4) A dictionary defines words. The Bible defines sin and righteousness. (5) A lamp lights our path. The Bible shines the light of truth. (6) Honey is sweet to taste and gives us energy. The Bible brings us joy and gives us spiritual life.

Verses to consider

Psalm 119:11—Thy word have I hid in mine heart, that I might not sin against thee.

Psalm 119:103—How sweet are thy words unto my taste! yea, sweeter than honey to my mouth!

Psalm 119:105—Thy word is a lamp unto my feet, and a light unto my path.

2 Timothy 3:16—All scripture is given by inspiration of God, and is profitable for doctrine, for reproof, for correction, for instruction in righteousness.

Applications

1. The Bible contains many good things. It is necessary to read and study it.
2. Without the Bible, life is a puzzle, a dark place, a winding road, and an unpleasant experience.
3. Bible memory puts the powerful Word of God into our hearts.

Additional ideas

1. You can take a trip with the Bible. Start down the road and you will come to crossroads. Find a Scripture verse to tell us which way to go. These ideas will get you started:

- Honesty one way and dishonesty the other: Proverbs 12:22.

- Anger one way and forgiveness the other: James 1:19, 20.

- Temptation one way and fleeing the other: Ephesians 4:27; 2 Timothy 2:22.

- It is time to work, but I'm feeling lazy: Proverbs 6:6-11; Proverbs 10:4.

- I hear a rumor about someone: Proverbs 11:13; James 4:11.

- I don't like what my authority just told me: Hebrews 13:17; Romans 13:1.

Sin and Its Scars

Theme

Sin can be forgiven, but sometimes it leaves scars.

Items you will need

○ A piece of stiff paper (card stock)
○ A handful of pushpins

Object lesson

Hold the paper so everyone can see it. Tell them the paper represents our hearts, fresh and clean. Explain that when we sin it is like pushing a pin into the paper. List various sins as you push the pins into the card stock: lying, stealing, unkindness, disobedience.

The pushpins are on our record. We must confess our sins, and God will forgive us. Pull the pins out to show that we are forgiven. The pushpins can be pulled out, but there are scars left behind. Even after we've been forgiven and our sins are taken away, we may still carry the scars of our wrongdoing.

Some consequences for sin might be receiving punishment or making restitution.

Verses to consider

Genesis 3:8-12—Adam and Eve's sin and the resulting scars of sin.

Genesis 4—Cain's scar for murdering Abel.

*1 Timothy 1:15—*This is a faithful saying, and worthy of all acceptation, that Christ Jesus came into the world to save sinners; of whom I am chief.

Applications

1. We must be careful to do only what's right so we can avoid scars.
2. Scars can be the remembrance of a bad deed we did. We live with those memories. Others may remember us for the bad deed.
3. Sometimes because of carelessness or disobedience, we hurt ourselves, and we carry that physical condition with us through life. Playing with fire can result in burns that leave lasting scars.
4. Another scar we can carry is the remembrance of physical harm we brought to others in our folly. For example, shooting someone with a BB gun or slingshot could leave them blind in one eye.

Additional ideas

1. You can ask the children to show you a scar on their hands or faces. Ask them the story behind them.
2. Tell a story of a scar you carry.
3. Perhaps there is a tree close by that has a scar in its bark that you can use for an example.

Following Instructions

Theme

We should follow instructions carefully.

Items you will need

○ Two combination locks

Object lesson

Write the instructions on the board for how to open a lock. Have a volunteer try his hand at opening it. Or take two combination locks and write up the instructions for each one. Have two volunteers race to see who can get their lock open first.

Often we're tempted to run ahead and try something quickly. The results are better if we slow down and follow each step correctly. We find blessing in following God's way. If we do things our way instead of following His instructions, we will still be locked away from Him, just as the combination lock stays closed until we follow the directions.

Verses to consider

Proverbs 1:7—The fear of the LORD is the beginning of knowledge: but fools despise wisdom and instruction.

Proverbs 4:1—Hear, ye children, the instruction of a father, and attend to know understanding.

Deuteronomy 28:1, 2—And it shall come to pass, if thou shalt hearken diligently unto the voice of the LORD thy God, to observe and to do all his commandments which I command thee this day, that the LORD thy God will set thee on high above all nations of the earth: and all these blessings shall come on thee, and overtake thee, if thou shalt hearken unto the voice of the LORD thy God.

Applications

1. We must pay close attention to details and instructions in life.
2. Carefulness in each step of a project pays in the end.
3. God wants us to pay careful attention to our parents' directions and to His Word.

Additional ideas

1. You can also use a paper-folding project, such as a paper airplane. Have some of the children try to copy what you are doing and follow your instructions. See how well their project turns out.
2. Tell a story of a disaster that occurred when someone didn't follow directions.

The Desire for More

Theme

Greed often leaves us empty and sad rather than filled and happy.

Items you will need

- A large bowl filled with Skittles or M&Ms
- Two cups
- Two spoons

Object lesson

Set the bowl of candy on a chair on one side of the room, and two cups on the other side of the room. Ask for two volunteers. Give them each a spoon and tell them to use it to carry candy from the bowl to their cup.

They may keep whatever candy they can get moved, but they must be quick because they will have only one minute. When you say *Stop!*, they must be at their cup to keep their candy. If they are caught somewhere in between, they lose their candy. Work it so that at least one of them is caught away from the bowl.

Call it greed or just plain wanting all we can get, the drive for more often gets us into trouble. So many times while chasing for more, we miss out on good things right now. Greed often ends in waste too—watch how much candy gets dropped on the floor!

To help ease the pain of losing the candy, have the volunteers pass candy out to the whole group. It is more blessed to give than to receive.

Verses to consider

Luke 12:15-21—The rich fool who laid up treasure for himself and never got to enjoy it.

Acts 20:35—I have shewed you all things, how that so labouring ye ought to support the weak, and to remember the words of the Lord Jesus, how he said, It is more blessed to give than to receive.

Ephesians 4:28—Let him that stole steal no more: but rather let him labour, working with his hands the thing which is good, that he may have to give to him that needeth.

Applications

1. We must be careful not to be greedy.
2. True happiness comes in giving rather than getting.
3. Hording things for ourselves often becomes wasteful.
4. Haste often makes waste.
5. True, careful, hard work to provide for ourselves has God's blessing.

Additional ideas

1. You can also demonstrate how many more coins you can get in an open hand than in a clenched fist. Tell one person to grab all they can out of a container and then count the value. Have the same person hold their hand open while you pile on coins and see how many more they can hold in an open hand.

2. Tell them a story of someone you know who was greedy.

Time and Eternity

Theme

Time is short and eternity is long.

Items you will need

- A long rope, perhaps as long as the room you will be in
- Black or color tape on two inches of the end of the rope

Object lesson

Have some volunteers help you stretch out the rope. Tell them the rope represents eternity and the taped section represents a person's lifetime. Have the students imagine that the rope goes out the window and on and on.

Ponder the two inches of rope identified with tape as compared to eternity. Ask them to think about the oldest person they know. Is that a long time to them? Point out that all those years are represented by just the couple inches of tape at the one end of the rope.

Ask them how long the rope would need to be to represent how long eternity is. The rope would never end in either direction! That's beyond our comprehension. The decisions we make in the short section of taped rope affect where we spend the rest of the rope.

Verses to consider

Isaiah 57:15—For thus saith the high and lofty One that inhabiteth eternity, whose name is Holy; I dwell in the high and holy place, with him also that is of a contrite and humble spirit, to revive the spirit of the humble, and to revive the heart of the contrite ones.

Genesis 2:7—And the LORD God formed man of the dust of the ground, and breathed into his nostrils the breath of life; and man became a living soul.

Applications

1. Every person has a beginning but no end.
2. Every person will exist after death somewhere.
3. Time is our opportunity to prepare for a long eternity with God.
4. Imagine rejoicing with God in Heaven forever and ever and ever!

Additional ideas

1. You can use the same idea but color the middle of the rope to represent time. God has been from eternity past and will be on into eternity future. Time is just a small spot in the span of God's eternity.
2. You could also stretch a string around the perimeter of the room to illustrate this concept.

Loving Responses

Theme

Love triumphs over evil.

Items you will need

- Two balloons
- Long wooden skewer
- Vegetable oil

  Note: Practice this in advance to learn the proper amount of oil on the skewer and the proper amount of air in the balloons.

Object lesson

Fill two balloons with air (not too full) and tie them shut. Prick one balloon with a long wooden skewer—it will pop. Oil the skewer with vegetable oil and stick it through the other balloon starting near the thick rubber at the balloon opening and going out through the thick rubber at the opposite side. With oil on the skewer and by sticking it through the less-stretched ends, you can impale the balloon without it popping.

You can liken the oil to love, forbearance, and humility in relationships. You can also liken the oiled skewer to the grace of God in our lives, helping us to accept hurts and disappointments that pierce our hearts.

Verses to consider

John 13:34, 35—A new commandment I give unto you, That ye love one another; as I have loved you, that ye also love one another. By this shall all men know that ye are my disciples, if ye have love one to another.

Ephesians 4:15—But speaking the truth in love, may grow up into him in all things, which is the head, even Christ.

Proverbs 15:1—A soft answer turneth away wrath: but grievous words stir up anger.

Applications

1. Love is the oil that makes all relationships work much better.
2. When we speak the truth in love, it is so much easier for others to listen and learn.
3. Forbearance and humility will keep us from exploding when criticized by others.
4. Our attitudes—not what others do to us—will determine our responses.

Additional ideas

1. You could contrast Cain's and David's responses when rebuked.
2. You can use this lesson to illustrate that we don't need to let bad circumstances ruin our lives.

38

Encouragement

Theme

Encouragement makes life easier.

Items you will need

- A pair of rusty pliers (or other tool) that hardly opens
- A penetrating oil or lubricant of some sort

Object lesson

Liken the rusty pliers to how we might feel when things are difficult for us: we think we can't do what we need to because it's too hard. Liken the oil to encouragement from a friend.

Treat the pair of pliers with the oil and exercise it. Give a few more treatments, notice how they operate more smoothly with each treatment of encouragement.

Ask the students to think of ways we can encourage others. For example:

- Tell someone they are doing a good job.
- Tell someone you are praying for them.
- Ask someone if they need help.

- ○ Send a card or letter to them.
- ○ Give them a small gift.
- ○ Spend time with them.

Verses to consider

1 Samuel 23:16—And Jonathan Saul's son arose, and went to David into the wood, and strengthened his hand in God.

Isaiah 50:4—The Lord GOD hath given me the tongue of the learned, that I should know how to speak a word in season to him that is weary.

Proverbs 15:23—A man hath joy by the answer of his mouth: and a word spoken in due season, how good is it!

Proverbs 17:17—A friend loveth at all times, and a brother is born for adversity.

Applications

1. A word of encouragement can make a big difference for a weary person.
2. Life's difficulties and pains are lightened by the oil of joy and cheer.
3. Life naturally has some harsh elements that can make people weary and tempt them to despair.
4. A kind word of encouragement can rescue a person from despair and make them a useful tool again.

Additional ideas

1. You could also use this object lesson to teach what happens when we neglect something in our lives. It becomes "rusty" and needs help to improve. You could talk about bad habits that we allow to develop in our lives and how hard it is to correct them.

2. You could also contrast a rusty tool to a brand-new tool exactly like it. Will the rusty one ever be "like new" again? Sin leaves scars on lives. Jesus cleanses us from sin—hallelujah! But He has not promised to always remove remembrances or reaping the consequences of sin.

God Looks on the Heart

Theme

Sometimes when the outside looks good, the inside is bad.

Items you will need

- A good apple
- An apple with dark food coloring injected into it
- A knife and dish

Object lesson

Have the "bad" apple shined ahead of time; using a bit of wax can really get a shine on it. Have the "good" apple dull and maybe slightly scuffed, but still looking okay. Which is the better apple? Which would the children choose?

When you cut them open, you see something completely different from what the outside looked like. Cut the shiny apple first and show them the ugly heart inside. Then cut the dull apple and show them the beautiful heart inside.

The shiny apple deceived us because it looked so impressive on the outside. Sometimes people can be that way too. They look just right for everyone to see, but their hearts are not happy or kind. Or sometimes we might see someone who looks plain and boring, only to realize when we get to know him that he is a truly lovely person.

Verses to consider

1 Samuel 16:7—But the Lord said unto Samuel, Look not on his countenance, or on the height of his stature; because I have refused him: for the Lord seeth not as man seeth; for man looketh on the outward appearance, but the Lord looketh on the heart.

2 Corinthians 10:7—Do ye look on things after the outward appearance? If any man trust to himself that he is Christ's, let him of himself think this again, that, as he is Christ's, even so are we Christ's.

Acts 1:24—And they prayed, and said, Thou, Lord, which knowest the hearts of all men, shew whether of these two thou hast chosen.

Matthew 23:27—Woe unto you, scribes and Pharisees, hypocrites! for ye are like unto whited sepulchres, which indeed appear beautiful outward, but are within full of dead men's bones, and of all uncleanness.

Mark 4:22—For there is nothing hid, which shall not be manifested; neither was any thing kept secret, but that it should come abroad.

Applications

1. God knows what's inside our hearts even if we think we have it hidden.
2. Time will reveal what is in a person's heart.
3. A good person will be true to God, inside and out.
4. Covering sin is only temporary, and God will bring judgment by revealing it eventually.

Additional ideas

1. Tell a story of a time when you trusted someone you thought had a good character and discovered later they were "rotten" inside.
2. Tell about a time when someone trusted you, but you turned out to be untrustworthy.
3. You could use the story of Ananias and Sapphira to illustrate a hidden, bad heart being revealed by God.

Ye Have Done It Unto Me

Theme

We hurt Jesus when we hurt others.

Items you will need

○ A drawing of Jesus

○ A picture of someone different from your audi-
ence, for example, someone from another coun-
try or someone with a deformity or handicap
Note: Both the picture and drawing should be pasted
to cardboard to provide stiffness.

○ A screwdriver

Object lesson

Overlay the drawing of Jesus with the picture of the
person. You may want to tape the two together.

Hold up the picture of the person. Talk about the temptation to mock this person because of how he is different. As
you discuss things others might say to mock this person,
stab the picture with a screwdriver to illustrate how it hurts
his heart. Do this multiple times.

Pull the front picture away and reveal the drawing of Jesus. Explain how our hurtful words against others—even if they never hear them—hurt the Lord Jesus.

Verses to consider

Matthew 25:40—And the King shall answer and say unto them, Verily I say unto you, Inasmuch as ye have done it unto one of the least of these my brethren, ye have done it unto me.

Ephesians 4:32—And be ye kind one to another, tenderhearted, forgiving one another, even as God for Christ's sake hath forgiven you.

Proverbs 19:17—He that hath pity upon the poor lendeth unto the LORD; and that which he hath given will he pay him again.

Matthew 10:42—And whosoever shall give to drink unto one of these little ones a cup of cold water only in the name of a disciple, verily I say unto you, he shall in no wise lose his reward.

Matthew 7:12—Therefore all things whatsoever ye would that men should do to you, do ye even so to them: for this is the law and the prophets.

Applications

1. It hurts Jesus when we mistreat others. He sees everything we do.

2. On the other hand, when we do kind deeds of service to others, especially the poor and lowly, we are doing it to Jesus.
3. We should think about how others feel and treat them like we would want to be treated.

Additional ideas

1. The story of the Good Samaritan illustrates this truth (Luke 10:30-37).
2. Consider the story of the Shunammite woman who gave Elisha a room in her house (2 Kings 4).
3. Tell about a time when you were unkind to someone.
4. You could also add another element with a positive response to a poor person and then reveal a smiling Jesus behind the poor person.

Christian Light is a nonprofit, conservative Mennonite publishing company providing Christ-centered, Biblical literature including books, Gospel tracts, Sunday school materials, summer Bible school materials, and a full curriculum for Christian day schools and homeschools. Though produced primarily in English, some books, tracts, and school materials are also available in Spanish.

For more information about the ministry of Christian Light or its publications, or for spiritual help, please contact us at:

ADDRESS :: P. O. Box 1212,
Harrisonburg, VA 22803
TELEPHONE :: 540-434-0768
FAX :: 540-433-8896
E-MAIL :: info@christianlight.org
WEBSITE :: www.christianlight.org

CHRISTIAN LIGHT
PUBLICATIONS